W9-AJS-494

Killer Bees

A Dillon Remarkable Animals Book

Killer Bees

By Kathleen Davis
and Dave Mayes

 **DILLON PRESS**
New York

Maxwell Macmillan Canada
Toronto

Maxwell Macmillan International
New York   Oxford   Singapore   Sydney

NORTHPORT PUBLIC LIBRARY
NORTHPORT, NEW YORK

Acknowledgments

Our sincere gratitude goes to Anita Collins, PhD., research leader for the U.S. Department of Agriculture-Agricultural Research Service, Honey Bee Research Laboratory in Weslaco, Texas. Dr. Collins, who has worked with Africanized honey bees in Africa, South America, and the United States since 1976, graciously gave her expert advice and time to review the manuscript.

Photo Credits

Cover photo courtesy of Terry Urdell
Back cover photo courtesy of the United States Department of Agriculture-Agricultural Research Service
Terry Urdell: frontispiece, title page, 12, 19, 20, 22, 28; Paul Hudgins (illustrator): 8; William Adams: 15; United States Department of Agriculture-Agricultural Research Service: 17, 30, 33, 51; Blanca Jackson: 24; Electron Microscopy Center/Texas A&M University: 26, 49; Texas Agricultural Extension Service: 29, 39; Jerrold Summerline: 36; Kathleen Davis: 40, 54.

Book design by Carol Matsuyama

Library of Congress Cataloging-in-Publication Data

Davis, Kathleen,
    Killer bees / by Kathleen Davis and Dave Mayes. — 1st ed.
       p. cm. — (Remarkable animals)
    Includes index.
    Summary: Describes the origin, characteristics, behavior, and dangerous aspects of the hybrid honey bee that has been moving north from Brazil for nearly thirty years and has now entered Texas.
    ISBN 0-87518-582-7
    1. Africanized honey bee—Juvenile literature. 2. Africanized honey bee—United States —Juvenile literature. [1. Africanized honey bee. 2. Bees.] I. Mayes. Dave. II. Title. III. Series.
QL568.A6D36   1993

599.79'9—dc20
                                    92-46894

Copyright © 1993 by Kathleen Davis and Dave Mayes

All rights reserved. No part of this book may be reproduced or transmitted in any form or by any means, electronic or mechanical, including photocopying, recording, or by any information storage and retrieval system, without permission in writing from the Publisher.

Dillon Press
Macmillan Publishing Company
866 Third Avenue
New York, NY 10022

Maxwell Macmillan Canada, Inc.
1200 Eglinton Avenue East
Suite 200
Don Mills, Ontario M3C 3N1

Macmillan Publishing Company is part of the Maxwell Communication Group of Companies.
First edition
Printed in the United States of America
10 9 8 7 6 5 4 3 2 1

Contents

Facts about the Africanized "Killer" Honey Bee.....6

1. "Killer" Bees: How Dangerous Are They?.........9

2. Life in and around the Colony...........................21

3. Taking a Closer Look.....................................31

4. They're Here—Can We Live with Them?........41

Sources of Information about
the Africanized Honey Bee...................................56

Glossary..57

Index..59

Facts about the Africanized "Killer" Honey Bee

Scientific Name: *Apis mellifera scutellata* hybrid

Description:

Length of Body—About five-eighths of an inch (1.5 centimeters)

Physical Features—Fine hairs cover body and legs; pollen pouches on sides; stinger on females at end of abdomen; males have no stinger; the tarsi, or feet, sense noise as vibrations

Weight—About 3,500 bees equal one pound

Color—Yellow stripes around a black or dark brown abdomen

Distinctive Habits: Reacts to disturbances around hive within 30 seconds; can stay angry for days after being disturbed; is disturbed when people or animals come within 40 feet (12 meters) of hive; more individual bees will help attack after the first bee stings; is not picky about where hive is built as long as it is sheltered from sun and rain; swarms frequently

Food: Honey, which the bees make out of nectar from flowers, is a source of carbohydrates. Pollen, also from flowers, is a protein source fed to young bees. Honey bees also must have water, which they use to dilute the honey before eating it

Reproductive Cycle: There is only one queen in each colony. She mates only once in her life, but with many drones, or male bees. The four stages of a honey bee's life include egg, larva, pupa, and adult. It takes about 19 days for a regular worker bee to develop from an egg, 16 days for a queen, and 23 days for a drone

Life Span: Drones usually live five to ten weeks, workers live about 30 days, and a queen lives an average of three years

Range: The ancestors of the Africanized bee still live throughout Africa, south of the Sahara Desert. African bees were accidentally introduced into the wild in Brazil in 1956. They mated with European bees, and the hybrid, or "Africanized," bee has spread across South and Central America. The first Africanized bee was found in the United States in October 1990. The bees are expected to spread across the southern part of the country, where the winters are not harsh

From Africa to the Americas

Chapter 1

"Killer" Bees: How Dangerous Are They?

In *The Swarm*, a science fiction movie that is sometimes shown on television late at night, great clouds of angry bees attack entire cities and sting hundreds of people to death. These busy bees also send a train over a cliff, make helicopters crash, blow up a power plant, and burn Houston to the ground. Whew!

The film is pure baloney, but it has added to the folklore that has grown up over the last 30 years around a **race,*** or kind, of bee known as the **"killer" bee.** The bee's reputation, fueled by fear and half-truths, is that of a buzzing bogey beast—a giant bug so scary and mean that it delights in hunting victims down and stinging them hundreds of times.

The "killer" bee has a scary reputation—as this illustration from a Texas newspaper shows—but the insect is not as frightening as it seems.

*Words in **bold type** are explained in the glossary at the end of this book.

In real life, the "killer" bee is no six-legged monster. There is much about this insect that is greatly exaggerated. But like many legends, this one contains kernels of truth. On rare occasions, **swarms** of thousands of these bees have attacked people and animals and stung them to death.

Time magazine first called them killers in a frightening report about bee attacks in Brazil in 1965. Describing one swarm as a "buzzing mass that darkened the sun," the magazine reported that in three hours the bees had killed flocks of chickens and injured 500 people, including one man who had so many stingers in his bald head that he "thought he was growing hair again."

Attacks like these have proven to be rare. Usually the stingings involve one or two people—not one or two cities. A person who thinks quickly and runs fast usually can get away from "killer" bees. But some have died because they could not escape. A number of the victims have been small children and elderly people. Others have been stung hundreds of times while fleeing but survived. Many of the animals that died were held in a stall or on a rope at the time of the attack and couldn't run away.

No one knows exactly how many people the bees have killed in Brazil and other parts of South and Central America. It is not easy to gather such facts in the wild where the bees like to live, which is one reason why rumors about these insects can get out of hand. One respected estimate suggests that the bees might have killed as many as 1,000 people in 30 years. That sounds like a lot, but it's an average of about 33 people a year—fewer than the 40 who die in the United States each year from allergic reactions, for the most part, to stings of wasps, yellow jackets, and regular honey bees.

Honey Bees with an Attitude

"Killer" bees don't look like killers. They look just like other honey bees and in fact are a tiny bit smaller. They do act differently. "Killer" bees are much less tolerant of other creatures that come too near their nests. They will sense a threat sooner, become upset more quickly, and attack in greater numbers. In short, they are honey bees with an attitude and a temper.

Even so, like many other animals, these insects

"Killer" bees look just like ordinary honey bees, only a bit smaller.

become angry only when they think their young in **hives** are threatened. People can and do get along with these bees, especially once their behavior is better understood.

Here in the United States, we will be hearing a lot more about "killer" bees. The first swarms came into this country from Mexico in the fall of 1990, when they were found near Brownsville in the southern tip of Texas.

Entomologists, scientists who study insects, are unsure how far north the bees will range. Some scientists believe they will live throughout the nation. Others think that because the bees are used to living in the **tropics,** they may settle only in the warmer, southern states.

Bees from Brazil

The bees have been migrating through South and Central America since 1956, when they were imported, or brought, into Brazil from Africa. Some scientists then had hoped that these African bees would be much better producers of honey. But during an experiment, some African **queen bees** were accidentally released into the wild. They mated with other bees in the area, and their offspring thrived in the Brazilian jungles. The new **hybrid** bees became known as the **"Africanized" honey bees.** (Entomologists use this name because they consider it more accurate than "killer" bees.) Many of the Africanized bees, scientists soon found, were ill-tempered and angry—a **trait,** or behavior pattern, inherited from the African queens.

In the years that followed, scientists were surprised to discover that the Africanized bees quickly drove out the other, gentler honey bees. The Africanized bee is so well suited to a tropical **environment** that it is outdoing other honey bees for food and is producing many more young. Now numbering in the billions, the Africanized bee is becoming the honey bee most commonly found in Central and South America, a remarkable biological change in such a short amount of time.

An Africanized honey bee hive in South America, where the insect is thriving

Scientists believe this has happened in part because of the kind of bee the Africanized bee is displacing: the gentler **European honey bee**. It has only been in the last 350 years that any honey bees have lived in the Americas. All of them were introduced by European settlers. They brought races of bees from their homelands, bees that were much better **adapted** to, or at home in, cooler climates.

U.S. Beekeepers Worried

It is the Africanized bee's bad temper, coupled with its ability to dominate a region, that has U.S. beekeepers worried. Beekeepers are people who raise honey bees for a living. This is an important business in the United States, where $150 million in honey is produced every year.

As valuable as honey is, many beekeepers owe their livelihood to the **pollination** services that their bees provide. Of the three million colonies of honey bees owned by commercial beekeepers, about one-third are used to pollinate agricultural crops. In many cases, the beekeeper moves bee **colonies,** usually housed in white wooden boxes, by truck to a farmer's field where a crop is in flower. The bees carry pollen from flower to flower, which allows plants to produce seed and fruit. In this way, the work of the bees helps produce an estimated one-third of the foods on American tables.

Beekeepers worry that Africanized bees will make it hard to stay in business. They are concerned that

16

Honey bees, like this one pollinating an apple blossom, help produce about 90 different crops.

Africanized bees will get angry if their hives are moved about for pollination. They are unsure just how well these bees will make honey, especially if most of their honey isn't stored in combs but goes to feeding multitudes of young bees.

One hopeful sign is that beekeepers in Brazil report that they are learning ways to work with Africanized bees so that they will be good honey makers and pollinators.

As the Africanized bees move into the United States, there is lots of disagreement among beekeepers and scientists on what should be done about them. A big part of the problem is that no one knows how well the Africanized bee will adapt to the area, or how widely it will range.

Most agree that the bees are here to stay and that it would be impossible to try to drive them out. In fact, it would be most foolish to try to kill all bees the way some cities fog mosquitoes. This would only create a situation in which gentler bees would be hurt the most and driven out sooner by Africanized bees.

This researcher is studying the behavior of Africanized honey bees. Scientists and beekeepers in the United States hope to learn how to make the testy insects good honey makers and pollinators.

Yet a major worry is that some cities will take that kind of drastic action, especially after someone dies from an Africanized bee stinging.

People in the United States simply may have to learn to live with Africanized bees, just as people in Latin American countries have done—without major difficulties—for years.

19

Chapter 2

Life in and around the Colony

Like other honey bees, Africanized bees are social insects. This means that they live in communities rather than by themselves. All honey bees in a colony have jobs that they must do to keep their home, the hive, healthy.

During a life span of about three years, the queen lays all the eggs that develop into new bees. During the height of the rearing season each year, the Africanized queen lays between 3,000 and 6,000 eggs a day—about twice as many as the European queen produces. The queen puts each egg into a separate cell of the **honeycomb.** Three days later, the egg hatches into larva. The nurse bee brings a honeylike food to the larva for about six days, then the cell is sealed with wax so the larva can finish developing

Surrounded by busy members of her colony is the queen bee. Her body is slightly longer than the others. Researchers have clipped one of her wings to prevent her from flying, and they have marked her with a bit of pink paint to easily identify her.

In this comb, developing bees are underneath the wax-sealed cells. The seals that appear thicker are drone cells, the ones from which the male bees will develop.

into a pupa and then into an adult bee. Africanized bees develop in about 19 days—one day less than European bees.

When the queen gets old, the **worker bees** know that it is time to raise a new queen. They choose a regular worker egg but give it more cells to grow in and make a special milky liquid for it to eat. With all the special attention, the queen matures in less time than other bees in the hive. When the queen is about one week old, it leaves the hive to mate.

In its life, the queen mates only once but with many males, or **drones**. During the mating flight, the queen collects sperm—the cells that fertilize eggs—

from each of the drones. The drones die after mating. The queen stores millions of sperm in the **spermatheca,** a sac in her body, until needed during egg laying.

Worker bees are responsible for all the chores that have to be done. Worker bees are females, but they are unable to lay eggs. They feed the young, forage for food, fan the hive to keep it cool, and scout for new nesting sites. One of the most important jobs in a hive is that of the **guards,** the worker bees responsible for protecting the nest. Africanized colonies have many more guard bees than European hives do, and Africanized guards never rest while standing watch over the hive's entrance.

When the guard bees sense trouble, they rally for an attack in less than 30 seconds. It takes European bees longer, about 45 seconds. Once the attack has begun, Africanized bees may stay angry for days, while European bees usually calm down in a few hours.

Africanized honey bees seem almost too active. Beekeepers familiar with European bees call the

Anatomy of the Worker Honey Bee

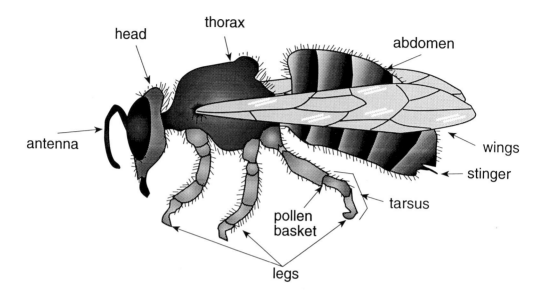

Africanized type "nervous." If a beekeeper tries to work with a colony of Africanized bees, for example, the bees will run all over, sometimes "parading" in big swooping groups. They also hang off the bottoms of combs in groups, called **festoons.** Calmer European bees usually continue to work on the comb or sit there quietly when a beekeeper works with their colony.

Like their European cousins, Africanized honey bees visit flowers to collect sweet nectar and pollen. They seem more jittery while visiting a flower and, because of their small size, carry a smaller load back to the colony. All honey bees use a dancing motion to tell their sisters in the hive where the good flowers are, but the Africanized bee dances less.

Covering a honey bee's black-and-yellow body is a fine coat of hair. Pollen that sticks to the hair is carried to another flower, where it brushes off. Thus the pollen grains from one flower fertilize, or pollinate, another, allowing that plant to produce fruit.

Home Sweet Hive

Everything that is dear to honey bees is contained within the walls of the hive: the queen, developing bees, drones, workers, and all the food. Naturally the bees want to protect their home, so they maintain a close watch.

No honey bee likes strangers, but Africanized honey bees are especially nervous about their hives. A person can walk to within a few feet of a European honey bee hive before the bees get upset. But Africanized honey bees may rally to fight if you get as close as 40 feet (12 meters).

The hairs on the abdomen of an Africanized bee provide an excellent way to trap grains of pollen as the bee moves about on flower petals. These hairs are 350 times their actual size.

The trouble is, wild honey bee hives blend so well with the surrounding plants and land that they may not be noticed until you already are too close. Spotting European honey bees is easier. Beekeepers provide neat white wooden boxes that act as high-rise apartments for domestic European honey bees. Wild European honey bees prefer to nest in a tree or other shelters away from the ground.

When Africanized honey bees choose a nesting site, they aren't picky. All they really want is protection from the sun and rain. A roomy white wooden box would be okay, but Africanized honey bees very often are found in hollow trees, holes in the ground, junk piles, water meters, and underneath mobile homes, for example.

That's one reason they pose a problem for us. Like many people, bees love luscious blooming plants. Yards stocked with flowers and plenty of water offer attractive nesting sites for the honey bees.

Honeycomb and Honey

From outside, the hives may appear different, but inside, the honeycomb walls of the Africanized and European bee hives are almost identical. Both types of honey bees make the comb from a liquid that comes out of glands on the worker bee's **abdomen,** or stomach area. The liquid hardens into wax scales that the bees form into **hexagonal,** or six-sided, cells. Within three days, the bees will have made enough comb for the queen to start laying eggs. The colony, which may number 60,000 bees, continues to build

Each bee on this honeycomb frame has a job to perform. Most of the cells have been sealed, but bright yellow pollen can be seen packed into some cells. Some bees are sticking their heads into a cell to either feed a developing bee or pack pollen. The whitish-looking cells are larvae.

comb as long as there is space. One Africanized hive found under a mobile home was more than six feet (about two meters) long.

Besides providing a place to raise new bees, the honeycomb cells are storage capsules for honey. Worker bees take nectar from flowers and carry it in the honey sac located inside their bodies. Nectar is about three-fourths water. The bees produce an **enzyme,** a kind of protein, that changes the nectar into honey. After storing the honey in cells, bees evaporate much of the water by fanning their wings. Then they put a layer of wax over the cells to seal the honey until it is needed.

28

An old irrigation pipe left in a pasture made a good place for Africanized bees to build comb.

Some people forget that the Africanized bee is a *honey* bee. In fact, some studies have shown that Africanized bees make a lot more honey than regular bees. But Africanized bees are not valued as honey producers for a couple of reasons. Instead of storing honey for a beekeeper to harvest, the Africanized bee uses much of its honey to feed developing bees. Then again, getting close to an Africanized bee hive is not an easy task!

Measuring the length of ten cells of a bee comb to learn whether it is Africanized

30

Chapter 3

Taking a Closer Look

If you see a honey bee land on a flower, you will not be able to tell whether it is an Africanized or European bee. A scientist faces the same problem. But entomologists need to know, if they are to offer good advice about coping with the Africanized bee.

Honeycomb offers one clue to scientists. Since the Africanized honey bee is slightly smaller than a regular honey bee, the Africanized cells also are tinier. When a wild hive is found, an inspector measures the length of ten cells. Ten cells from a regular honey bee comb usually measure about 2 inches (5.2 centimeters). Lower measurements may mean that the hive is Africanized and that lab tests are needed.

One of the most reliable and quickest lab tests is the Fast Africanized Bee Identification System, or

FABIS. It uses the measurements of the wings from worker bees to determine whether a sample of 12 bees from a colony is Africanized. The wings are mounted on a slide and projected on a screen for measurement. Because thousands of honey bees have been measured, scientists often can judge bees this way in a matter of minutes.

If a more accurate reading than FABIS is required, scientists in the lab will perform a **morphometrics** test. This test measures parts of the bees' bodies and compares them with information stored in a huge computer data base. A lab can have an answer about a sample within two hours.

Why So Defensive?

Africanized bees and European bees both have yellow stripes around a black or brown abdomen, and they are nearly the same size—about the width of a nickel. Color and size are traits that honey bees pass along from generation to generation through **genes** contained in their cells.

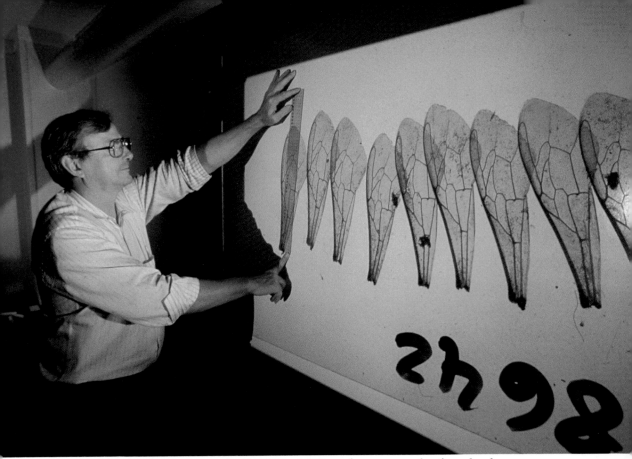

A scientist performs the FABIS test. Wings from a sample of worker bees are mounted on a slide and projected on a screen. A quick measurement tells whether the bees are Africanized.

Defensive behavior also is an inherited trait—one that appears strongly in Africanized bees. Things that normally do not bother a European honey bee, like a person walking past the hive, make an Africanized bee furious and highly defensive.

What makes the Africanized bee so defensive? It will take much more study to know for sure. But scientists think that its defensiveness stems from its

33

struggle to survive in the wild. For centuries these bees have had to compete for scarce food and water, raise huge numbers of young, and drive off numerous enemies. European bees, on the other hand, have been in the care of people for hundreds of years. European bees have been bred for gentleness and other traits that make them good honey producers. In a sense, then, we can think of European bees as the docile workhorses of the honey bee world, while their Africanized cousins are more the wild mustangs.

Absconding and Swarming

Perhaps because of their harsh life in the wild, Africanized bees have a strong survival **instinct**. European bees have been known to run out of food in the winter, and rather than leave home to search for a better place, the entire colony dies of starvation. Africanized honey bees would never allow that. When the honey supply runs low or the water source evaporates, the entire Africanized bee colony **absconds,** or leaves, to either find a better place or die trying.

Sometimes most of the bees leave the nest but a new queen and some of the workers stay behind with the young. Africanized bees can travel more than 100 miles (160 kilometers) at a time looking for better living conditions. This mass emigration in search of a new home is called swarming. Honey bees swarm when there are too many bees in the hive and not enough room to build more comb. Beekeepers try not to let their European bees swarm by controlling the number of developing bees and by providing extra space for growth.

But Africanized bees continue to develop new bees until the nest can't grow any larger. Then the old queen leads the swarm to a new location that scout bees have selected, and a new hive is built. The scout bees give off an orientation **pheromone,** a chemical that smells like lemons, to direct bees from their hive to the new location. Africanized bee colonies swarm about once every two months, perhaps flying for 10

Sometimes swarming bees land to rest on a tree limb.

miles (16 kilometers) before landing. European bees, if they swarm at all, only do so about once a year and then travel no more than 3 miles (5 kilometers).

Swarms look frightening—a large ball of bees hanging on a limb or flying in a tight, buzzing cloud. The workers "ball up" around the queen, following and protecting her. Even so, swarms of honey bees are usually the least threatening to humans. Because they do not have a home or young bees to defend, the bees are less likely to sting.

Bee Stings

Most people know two things about bees: They make honey and they can sting. An Africanized honey bee's sting is no worse than that of a regular honey bee. The **venom** from both is chemically the same, so stinging victims have the same physical reaction.

But Africanized bees are more sensitive to disturbances, and they quickly tell one another what is happening by releasing an alarm pheromone that smells like bananas. That is how a guard bee gets other bees to help with a stinging attack.

Africanized honey bees seem to pay more attention to the alarm pheromone than regular bees do. We don't know why, but scientists believe Africanized guard bees may release the alarm pheromone right at the hive entrance rather than in the air. Or it could be that more of the pheromone is released by Africanized bees than by regular bees. Whatever the reason, the alarm pheromone from Africanized bees results in an explosion of bees coming to the defense. A victim can receive hundreds of stings in two minutes.

Unlike other stinging insects such as yellow jackets, hornets, and wasps, honey bees can sting only once. The stinger on the worker bee has barbs on each side that stick in the skin. The sting shaft is a hollow tube through which the venom flows. When the stinger pierces the skin, the muscle that joins the stinger to the bee's abdomen causes a digging motion to work the barbs in deeper.

As the bee tries to free itself, the muscle pulls away from the body and remains with the stinger. With the body torn, the bee bleeds to death, usually within two hours. But the muscle attached to the barbed shaft continues to pump venom into the victim unless the stinger is removed. The venom sac can pump up to ten minutes. Stingers should be removed in a sideways scraping motion. If the stinger is tweezed or pinched out, that will squirt the remaining venom into the victim.

After a honey bee stings, the stinger is pulled away from the body and the bee bleeds to death.

How many bee stings can kill a person? Just one, if the person has an allergic reaction to honey bee venom. Fewer than one person in 100 has this condition, however. Most of us will experience some swelling, pain, and itching around the sting and nothing more.

As a rule of thumb, the body can withstand up to ten bee stings for every one pound of weight. In other words, a healthy 150-pound (68-kilogram) person may take up to 1,500 bee stings before going into toxic shock.

The stinger is the honey bee's weapon for defending the home front, and the Africanized bee uses it with vigor.

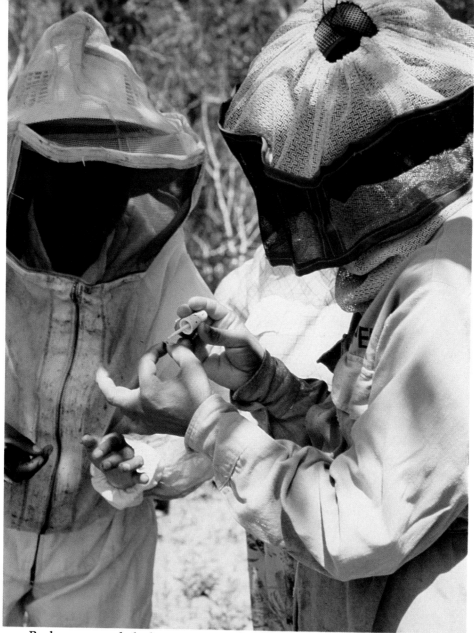

Beekeepers mark the back of a European queen with a dot of paint. They will mark all their European queens in this way to prevent Africanized bees from taking over their European hives. Any unmarked queens will be killed.

Chapter 4

They're Here— Can We Live with Them?

On May 20, 1991, a Brownsville, Texas, maintenance man was riding a lawn mower at a mobile home park when he passed by a driveway drainpipe.

Within seconds, Cenobio Jesus Diaz had bees all over him.

"Thousands of them followed me. . . . I was scared. . . .They followed me a long way, for about 250 feet."

Mr. Diaz, 35, suffered 18 stings on the right side of his head and hand. He was treated at a hospital— and given a small dose of national fame.

That week, news of his encounter with the bees was carried around the country. Mr. Diaz was heralded as the first person to be stung by Africanized bees in the United States.

It seems certain now that millions of colonies of Africanized bees will move into the southern United States from Mexico. The testy insect has sent entomologists scrambling for answers to a number of interesting questions.

Chief among them is this: Will the Africanized bee become more European—and therefore more gentle—as it moves farther north?

The answer will be important, for it will determine how defensive these insects will be, how far they will range, and how much of a problem they will be for the country's beekeepers, farmers, and people in general.

A Kinder, Gentler Bee?

Entomologists had hoped that Africanized bees would grow gentler as they interbred with the more docile bees found in Central America and Mexico. To buy time for this to happen in Mexico, the U.S. Department of Agriculture between 1987 and 1990 helped to

Projected Distribution of the Africanized Honey Bee in the United States

N

■ Current distribution
■ Anticipated distribution

kill more than 23,000 swarms of Africanized bees.

Did this idea work? Entomologists don't agree. Scientists who studied 85 wild bee swarms found very little evidence of genetic mixing. Other scientists, however, say that more studies must be done to be sure.

Most entomologists do agree that more genetic mixing or hybridization will take place in the United States. To survive, all animals must adapt to the climates they live in, and the United States has cold winters that will be very hard on tropical Africanized bees.

Because they are not as adaptive to cold weather as European bees, Africanized bees are unlikely to become the dominant bee throughout the country. Some scientists, however, suggest the Africanized bee will be able to survive all the way to Canada. Others believe that it may travel that far north in mild years but die back in years with very cold winters.

Africanized bees likely will become well established in the warm southern parts of the United

States, with European bees continuing to thrive in the colder north. A "hybrid zone" stretching across the American continent may develop between the two races.

One scientist has reported finding several such zones in South America, where the hybrids had both European and Africanized traits. For example, some Africanized bees were found to be as gentle as European bees. Other European colonies were as ill-tempered as Africanized ones.

Thus far in the United States, the Africanized honey bee has moved mostly along waterways, up the Gulf Coast, and along the Rio Grande, which separates Texas and Mexico. Scientists do agree that the combination of water and food sources will determine where the bee can live.

Clipping Wings and Quarantines

In Texas, beekeepers are working hard to prevent Africanized bees from taking over their European hives. They do this by ensuring that the queens are of

European stock. To make sure the right queens are laying eggs that develop as gentle bees, the beekeepers clip the wings of their European queens or mark their backs with a dot of paint or nail polish. Any unmarked queens found are killed.

The state has **quarantined** the counties in South Texas where the Africanized bee has been found. This prevents beekeepers from moving their commercial hives out of the quarantine zone without having them first certified, or approved, by a state inspector as being free of Africanized bees. In this way, the state is trying to prevent people from helping the spread of Africanized bees.

A technique called "drone flooding" is being tested by scientists in Guatemala. It also may help beekeepers maintain European bloodlines in Africanized areas. Because each queen can mate with many drones during her mating flight, any contact with Africanized drones will result in some portion of the colony becoming Africanized. Scientists have found that releasing large numbers of European drones during mating season could ensure European matings 95 percent of the time.

Coping with Africanized Bees

While some scientists are working on ways to slow down the numbers of Africanized bees being bred, others are working on ways to cope with the bees already in the United States.

For example, Dr. Anita Collins, a bee researcher in South Texas, is experimenting with a chemical that seems to repel bees temporarily. In early tests, Dr. Collins found that the chemical sprayed into the air stopped honey bees from stinging. The bees eventually recovered but not before giving a person time to get away. She also found, however, that spraying the chemical on clothing or skin did not repel bees at all.

Scientists don't know what the compound does to the bees in the air, and it must be tested further. But such a product may come in handy for people like telephone linemen, whose work may bring them into regular contact with Africanized bees.

Such a bee bomb would also be useful for people operating mowers or equipment outdoors, where attacks by Africanized bees have most often occurred. Since May 1991, some 120 stinging incidents have been reported in Texas. One of the most serious cases involved Mrs. Dorothy Byrd of Santa Rosa. Mrs. Byrd was using a trimmer to cut weeds around her daughter's mobile home when bees by the thousands boiled up from large honeycombs built under the house.

"All of a sudden, my head was covered with bees," Mrs. Byrd told news reporters. "All I kept screaming was, 'Get me help!' There was no way to get away from them."

Police rescued her by lighting road flares to drive the insects away. Mrs. Byrd was stung 400 times and spent three days recovering in a hospital.

Scientists believe it isn't the sound of engines and motors that is so upsetting to the bees. Bees actually don't "hear" sounds carried through the air. But they

Bees pick up vibrations with their sensitive feet. In this picture, an Africanized bee's front leg and clawlike foot have been magnified 200 times.

do have extremely sensitive feet, or tarsi, that pick up vibrations. The louder the sound, the greater the vibrations, and the more upset bees—especially Africanized ones—can become.

Dr. Hayward Spangler, an entomologist, is developing a device called a Stingometer that measures the number of stings received from angry bees in ten-second time periods. The Stingometer is a black plastic bottle with a sensor inside that counts how many times bees hit the bottle trying to sting it.

In a trial with Africanized bees in Costa Rica, Dr. Spangler found that his device recorded up to 24 hits per second. By comparison, tests with European bees in Arizona averaged about 4 hits per second.

When completed, the Stingometer could be placed at the entrance of a hive, where the bees would see it as a threat. It would be a quick way to learn whether a colony of bees might be Africanized.

Bee Trapping

Entomologists in Texas are working hard to track the northward spread of Africanized bees. It's important to know where the bees are headed so that people in their path can be prepared.

The bee is tracked with "traps." Usually these traps are nothing more than cardboard boxes covered with blue protective plastic and hung in trees. The traps are "baited" with a liquid similiar to the pheromone that directs a swarm looking for a home.

In Texas, more than 1,200 bee traps have been hung along hundreds of miles of roadways. Other states that anticipate the arrival of Africanized honey bees, such as New Mexico and Florida, have installed trap lines, too. Typically, crews check the boxes once

Scientists try out the Stingometer, a plastic bottle with a sensor inside that counts how many times bees hit the bottle every ten seconds.

or twice a month, depending on how actively the bees are swarming.

A hive of bees found in a box sometimes is given a defensiveness test. An alarm pheromone is sprayed into the box, making the bees upset and angry. After 30 seconds, the box is rapped sharply with a long pole. After another 30-second wait, a trapper waves a small patch of dark suede in front of the hive's entrance hole and counts the number of stings the cloth absorbs in two minutes. Usually a high number of stings—more than 100—suggests an Africanized colony.

The bee box then is taken down from the tree, the entrance hole covered, and the bees inside sprayed with insecticide or soapy water. The water "drowns" the bees after the soap dissolves the waxy coating on their bodies. They usually die within ten minutes.

On the ground, the crew measures the honeycomb and takes a number of field tests and measurements. Information gathered about Africanized bees from the traps helps state and local authorities know what and when to tell their citizens about the bee. Government officials want everyone to learn how to live with the bees and protect themselves from them. Some schools have started programs to teach young children to learn how to avoid being stung by the bees.

Africanized Bees and the Future

How much of a problem will Africanized bees become in the United States? We just don't know yet. So much depends on how far north the bee spreads and what kind of bee it becomes as it interbreeds with larger concentrations of European bees. If the bee keeps its bad temper and overruns the southern half of the United States, it will become a costly problem in a number of ways:

- The beekeeping industry will be the hardest hit. Beekeepers in Africanized areas will have to take expensive steps to maintain their European hives, or else learn how to manage Africanized bees. In the meantime, honey production may slow down.

In Texas, schoolchildren are given special lessons to learn how to live with the Africanized honey bee.

- Beekeeper pollination services will become more expensive to the farmer, driving up the costs of some fruits and vegetables.
- Local governments will have to educate their citizens about the bee and train their emergency response teams on how to cope with stinging incidents.
- More bee stingings will occur, and a few people and numerous animals will be killed.

Wherever the bee settles in the United States, people will pretty much be able to carry on their everyday lives as usual. This has been true in every other country that the bee has moved into in South and Central America.

Children won't have to dress like beekeepers— wear thick clothes with heavy gloves and screened headgear—when they go outside to catch the school bus or play ball. Picnics in the park won't require folks to eat in their cars with the windows rolled up.

And, unlike the scenes in some science fiction movies, Africanized bees won't attack entire cities, blow anything up, or make even one train jump the tracks.

The problems presented by the Africanized bee will provide a great opportunity for entomologists to expand their knowledge of the honey bee. As a result, all of us should gain a better understanding of this remarkable animal and the world that we share with it.

Sources of Information about the Africanized Honey Bee

To obtain a teaching kit:
People who are interested in teaching others about living with the Africanized honey bee in the United States may order a kit for $50 from the Texas Agricultural Extension Service. The kit contains lesson plans, color posters, a slide show with a script and cassette, a video, scratch 'n' sniff stickers, honeycomb, Africanized and European bees cast in plastic, and several brochures. Write to:

> Bee Kits
> TAES, Room 201
> Reed McDonald Building
> Texas A&M University
> College Station, TX 77843-2112

For information about the location of Africanized honey bees in the United States, write to:

> Kim Kaplan
> Public Affairs Specialist
> U.S. Department of Agriculture-Agricultural Research Service
> 10300 Baltimore Avenue
> BARC-West
> Beltsville, MD 20705-2350

For information about the Africanized honey bee in Texas, write:

> News and Public Affairs
> Department of Agricultural Communications, Room 203
> Reed McDonald Building
> Texas A&M University
> College Station, TX 77843-2112

Information about honey bees in general may be obtained from:

> National Honey Board
> 421 21st Avenue No. 203
> Longmont, CO 80501-1421

Glossary

abdomen (AB-duh-min)—the rear part of the body of an insect

absconding (ab-SKOND-ing)—when an entire colony of bees leaves its nest in search of a new place to live

adapt—to change to fit certain conditions, such as climate

Africanized honey bees—hybrids that are the result of matings between African bees and European bees

colony—a community of several thousand worker bees, usually with one queen; a colony may or may not contain drones

drones—male bees, which lack stingers

entomologist (ent-uh-MAHL-uh-jist)—a scientist who studies insects

environment—the air, the water, the soil, and all the other things that surround a person, animal, or plant

enzyme (EN-zime)—a protein produced by cells that helps cause specific chemical changes

European honey bee—race of bees brought to the Americas from Europe; the primary bee living in the United States

FABIS—Fast Africanized Bee Identification System, which takes measurements of wings of worker bees to determine if they are Africanized bees

festoon—a group of bees that link their legs and hang together, usually off the bottoms of combs

gene—the basic unit of inheritance found in living cells

guard bees—bees in a colony whose job is to protect the hive

hexagonal (hek-SAG-un-ul)—six-sided

hive—a nest, usually protected from weather, where bees have built honeycomb and begun raising young

honeycomb—a structure with hexagonal cells of beeswax built by bees for storing nectar, pollen, honey, and developing bees

hybrid (HI-brid)—the offspring of genetically different parents

instinct (IN-stinkt)—a way of acting or behaving that an animal is born with and does not have to learn

"killer" bees—exaggerated term for Africanized bees

morphometrics (more-fuh-MEH-triks)—the measurement of the form, or any of the parts, of an organism

pheromone (FUR-uh-mone)—a substance released by one bee that influences another bee to behave in a certain way

pollination (pol-uh-NAY-shun)—transfer of pollen, often assisted by bees, from one flowering plant to another, enabling it to bear fruit

quarantine (KWAR-un-teen)—to keep apart or isolate

queen bee—the female bee in the colony that lays all the eggs

race—a group of animals that share similar characteristics; a kind or breed of bee

spermatheca—a sac in a queen bee's body that stores sperm until needed during egg laying

swarm—a colony of bees actively looking for a new hive

trait—an inherited characteristic

tropics—a region of the earth that is near the equator; it is always warm in the tropics

venom (VEN-um)—a poisonous liquid

worker bees—female bees that cannot lay eggs but that perform nearly all the other jobs required in a colony

Index

Africa, 13

beekeepers, 16, 18, 23, 24, 26, 29, 35, 42, 45, 46, 53, 54, 55
Brazil, 10, 11, 13, 18
Byrd, Mrs. Dorothy, 48

Collins, Dr. Anita, 47
color, 25, 32
coping and living with "killer bees", 19, 31, 47, 53, 54

defensive behavior, 23, 25, 33, 42, 52
Diaz, Cenobio Jesus, 41
drone flooding, 46
drones, 22, 23, 25, 46, 47

eggs, 21, 22, 23, 27, 46
entomologists, 14, 31, 42, 44, 49, 50, 55
European honey bees, 15, 23-26, 31-36, 42, 44-46, 49, 53

Fast Africanized Bee Identification System (FABIS), 31, 32
feet (tarsi), 49
festoons, 24
food, 14, 25, 29, 34, 45

guard bees, 23, 37

hair, 25
hives, 13, 18, 21, 22, 23, 25, 27, 28, 29, 31, 33, 35, 37, 45, 46, 50, 52, 53
honey, 14, 16, 28, 29, 34, 37, 53
honeycomb, 21, 24, 27, 28, 31, 48, 52

hybridization, 44

mating, 22, 46, 47

nesting sites, 26, 27, 35

pheromone, 35, 37, 38, 50
pollen, 25
pollination, 16, 18, 25, 54

queen bees, 14, 21, 22, 23, 25, 27, 35, 36, 45, 46

size, 11, 24, 31, 32
Spangler, Dr. Hayward, 49
stingings, 9, 10, 11, 19, 37, 38, 39, 41, 47, 48, 49, 52, 54
Stingometer, 49, 50
Swarm, The, 9
swarms, 10, 13, 35, 36, 44, 50, 52

temper, 12, 14, 16, 23, 25, 45, 53
Texas, 13, 41, 45, 46, 47, 48, 50
traps, 50, 52

U.S. Department of Agriculture, 42
United States, 11, 13, 18, 19, 42, 44, 45, 53, 55

venom, 37, 38, 39
victims, 9, 10, 11, 37, 38, 39, 55

wings, 28, 32, 46
worker bees, 22, 23, 25, 27, 28, 35, 36, 38

Kathleen Davis is a science writer for the Department of Agricultural Communications at Texas A&M University. She was a newspaper reporter for 11 years and is the author of a book on the Civil War. She has a bachelor's and a master's degree in agricultural communications from Texas Tech University. Ms. Davis lives with her two children in College Station, Texas.

Dave Mayes directs the news operations for the Department of Agricultural Communications at Texas A&M University. He has been a writer and editor for more than 20 years, with most of his experience in daily newspaper journalism. He also has taught journalism at Texas A&M, where he helped establish a quarterly statewide public opinion poll. Mr. Mayes holds a bachelor's degree in journalism and a master's degree in urban planning. He lives with his wife and two children near Bryan, Texas.

$13.95

DATE			

MAR 1994

NORTHPORT-EAST NORTHPORT
PUBLIC LIBRARY
151 Laurel Avenue
Northport, NY 11768

BAKER & TAYLOR BOOKS